LES MISÉRABLES

FOR CLASSICAL PLAYERS

ISBN 978-1-5400-3755-8

To access companion recorded piano accompaniments online, visit:
www.halleonard.com/mylibrary

Enter Code
7772-8251-5683-3283

CONTENTS

At the End of the Day

Music by Claude-Michel Schönberg
Lyrics by Alain Boublil, Jean-Marc Natel
and Herbert Kretzmer

Bring Him Home

Music by Claude-Michel Schönberg
Lyrics by Herbert Kretzmer and Alain Boublil

Castle on a Cloud

Music by Claude-Michel Schönberg
Lyrics by Alain Boublil, Jean-Marc Natel
and Herbert Kretzmer

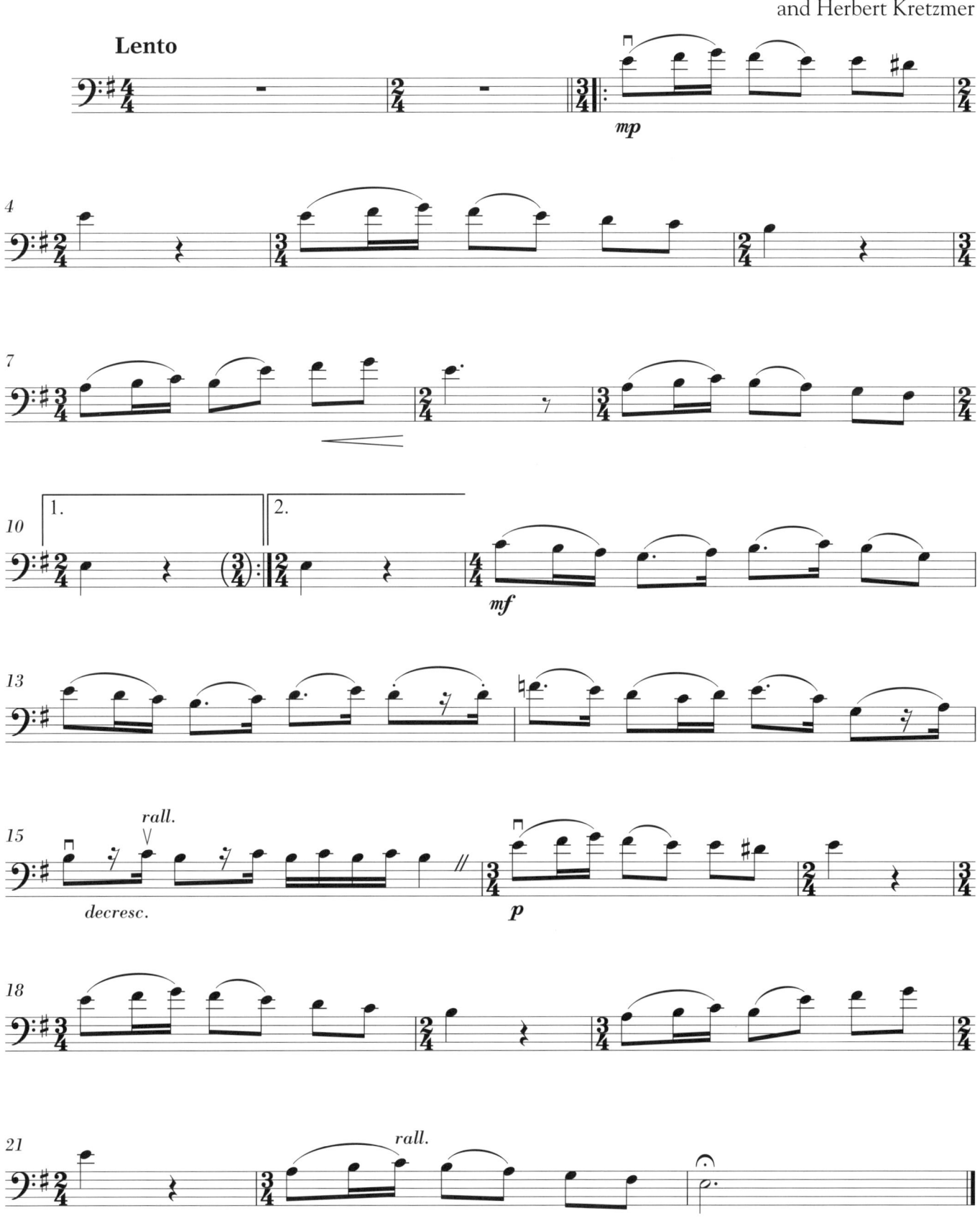

Do You Hear the People Sing?

Music by Claude-Michel Schönberg
Lyrics by Alain Boublil, Jean-Marc Natel
and Herbert Kretzmer

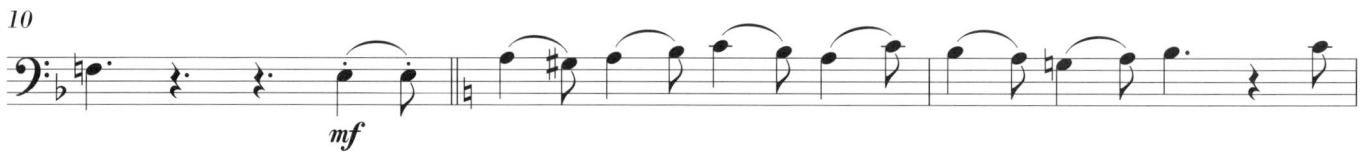

Maestoso

Drink with Me
(To Days Gone By)

Music by Claude-Michel Schönberg
Lyrics by Alain Boublil and Herbert Kretzmer

On My Own

Music by Claude-Michel Schönberg
Lyrics by Alain Boublil, Jean-Marc Natel,
Herbert Kretzmer, John Caird
and Trevor Nunn

Empty Chairs at Empty Tables

Music by Claude-Michel Schönberg
Lyrics by Alain Boublil and Herbert Kretzmer

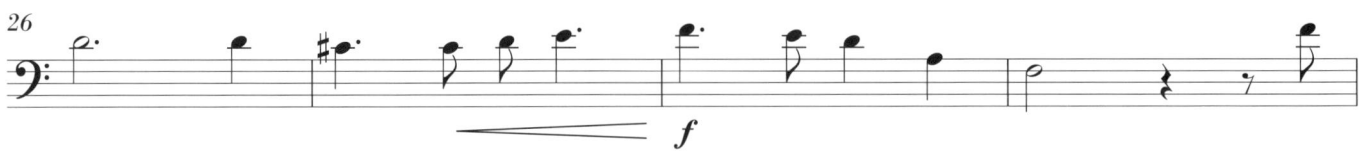

30
rall.
34
Tempo primo
38
42
Più mosso
46
decresc.
mp
50
accel.
rall.
f
Più mosso
54
molto rall.
mp
p
rall.
58
Tempo primo
rall.

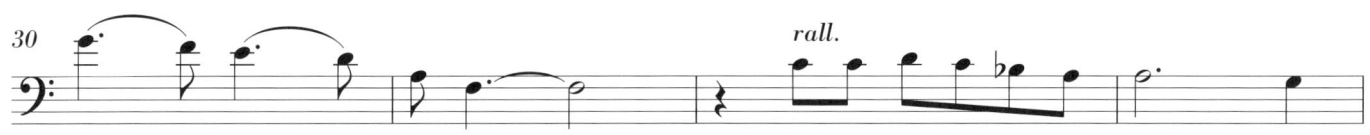

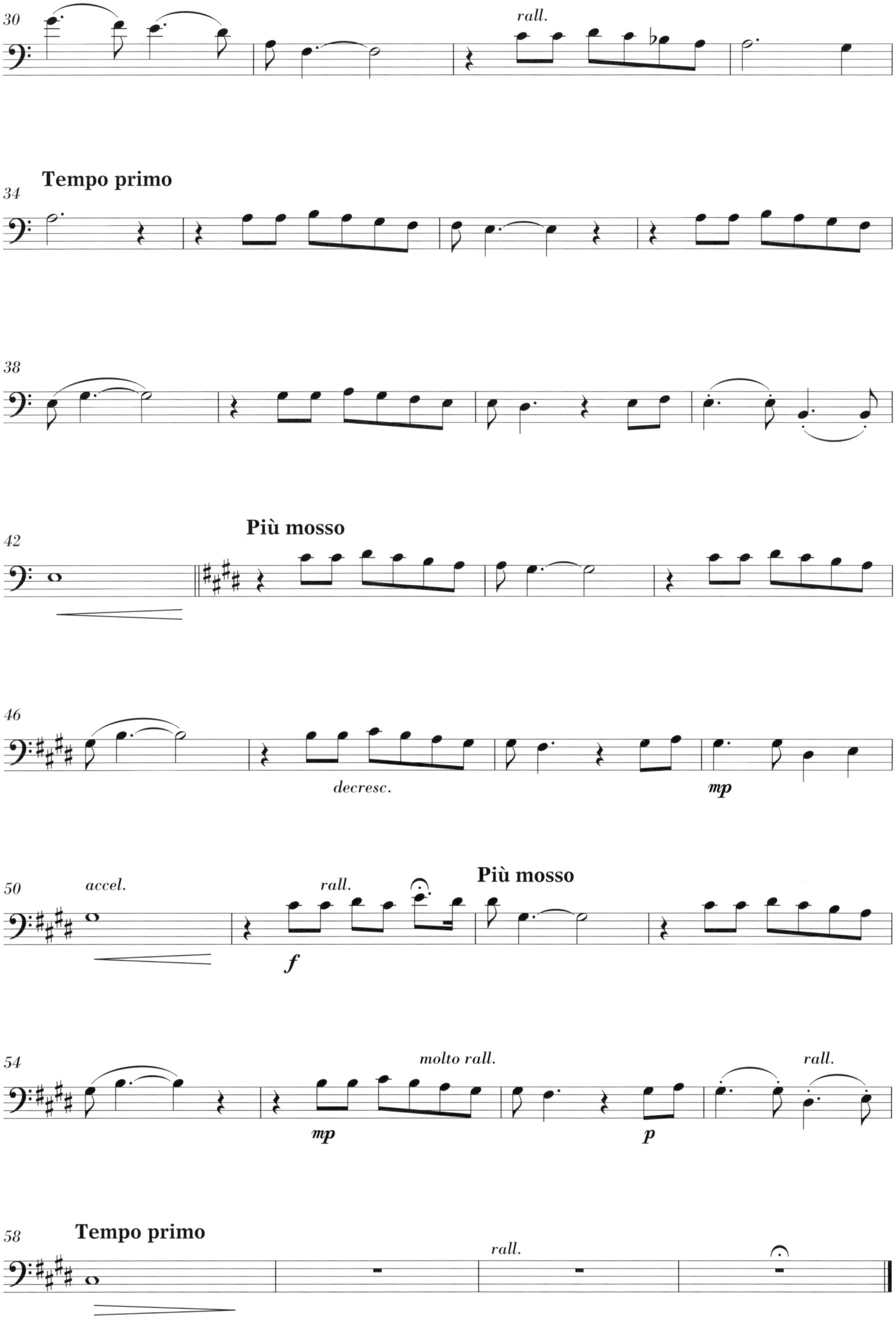

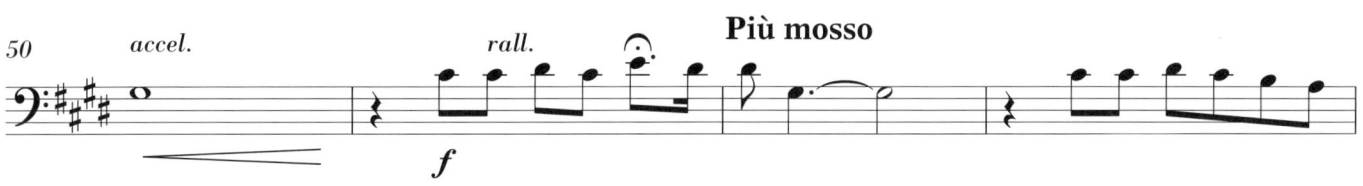

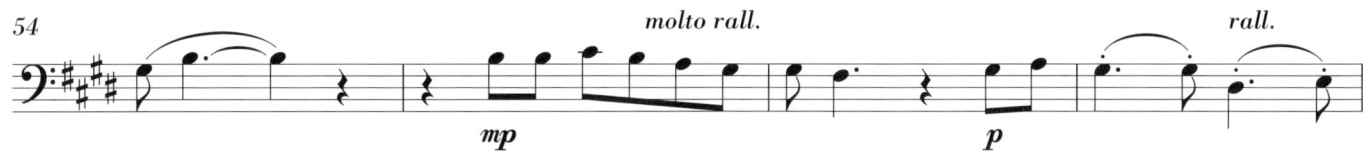

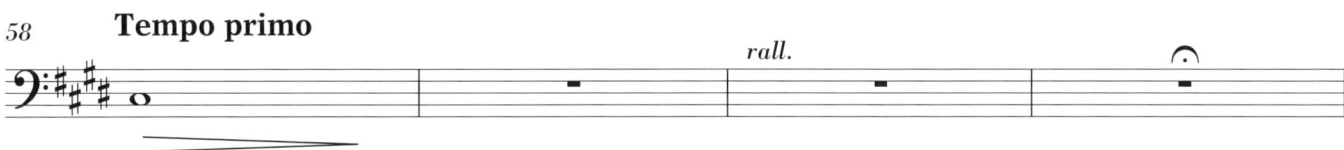

I Dreamed a Dream

Music by Claude-Michel Schönberg
Lyrics by Alain Boublil, Jean-Marc Natel
and Herbert Kretzmer

A Little Fall of Rain

Music by Claude-Michel Schönberg
Lyrics by Alain Boublil, Jean-Marc Natel
and Herbert Kretzmer

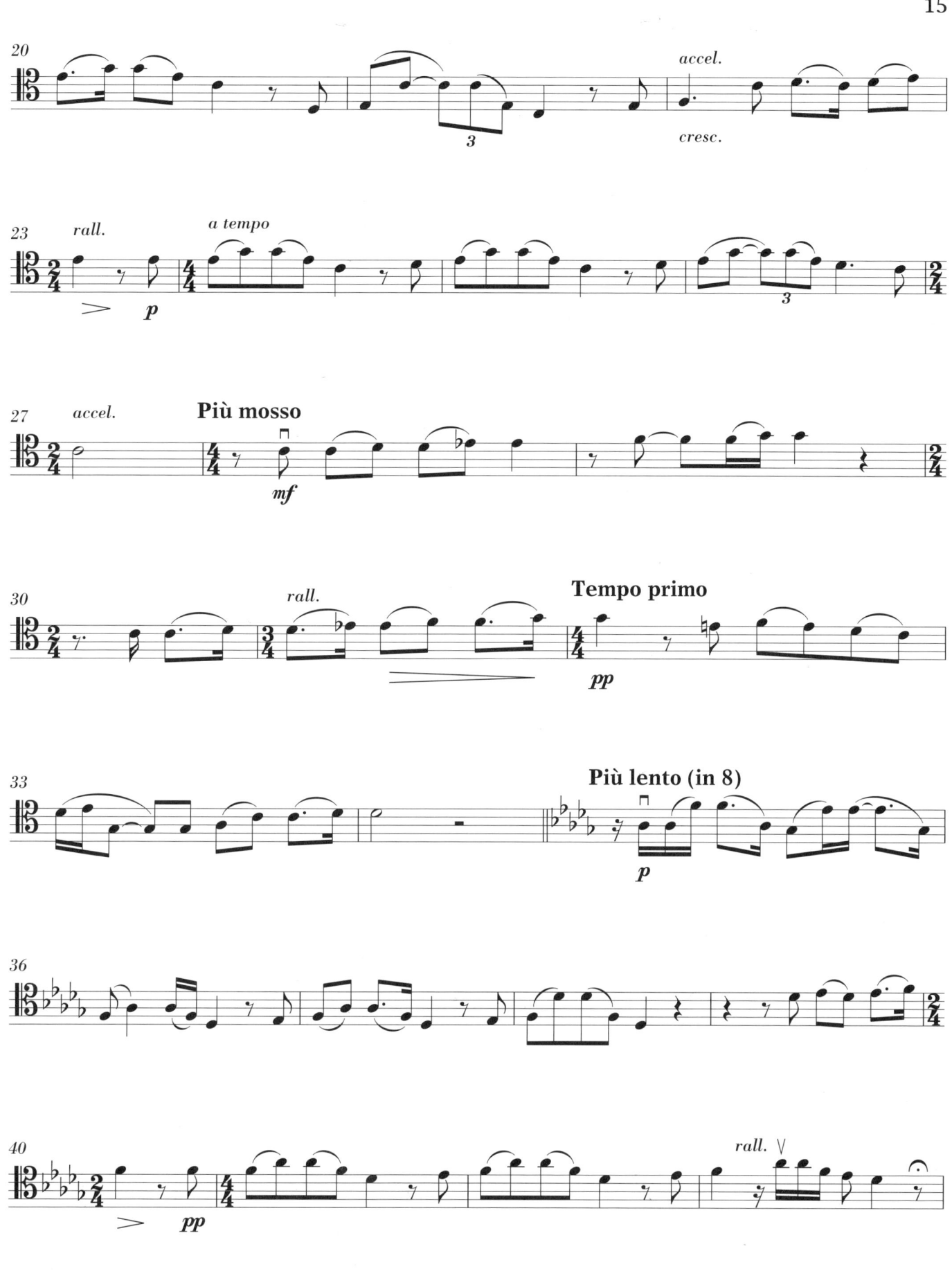

Stars

Music by Claude-Michel Schönberg
Lyrics by Herbert Kretzmer and Alain Boublil

The Thénardier Waltz of Treachery

Music by Claude-Michel Schönberg
Lyrics by Alain Boublil, Jean-Marc Natel
and Herbert Kretzmer

Who Am I?

Music by Claude-Michel Schönberg
Lyrics by Alain Boublil, Jean-Marc Natel
and Herbert Kretzmer